BEYOND NUMB

BEYOND NUMBERS

Empowering Business Owners Through Tax Planning

ISBN: 979-8-9885182-2-8

United States of America

Giants and Geniuses Publishing

Atlanta, GA

DEDICATION

To The Indomitable Business Owners,

In the ever-challenging world of entrepreneurship, your unwavering commitment and unyielding spirit inspire us. This book is dedicated to you, the lifeblood of our economy.

I recognize your daily struggles and triumphs. These pages offer insights, strategies, and knowledge to empower your journey. My mission is to help you navigate the intricate realm of taxation, enabling you to face tax bills confidently and avoid audits.

Your resilience in adversity, dedication to your businesses, and pursuit of excellence deserve our utmost respect. You are the true architects of innovation and progress.

May this book serve as a valuable resource, a guiding light, and a symbol of our support for your endeavors.

With Deepest Admiration,

Dr. Cozette M. White

ACKNOWLEDGEMENTS

To My Family,

Thanks for believing in me and your endless love and support. I am genuinely thankful to have you in my life.

To every client and mentee that has every trusted in me – thank you!

For those that have trusted me to mentor, coach, and empower them to gain clarity and focus on their finances.

It is my greatest prayer that this book will make a positive impact on your life.

Cozette

CONTENTS

You've opened your business, and you've spent your own money to keep your business up and running. You soon realize that you are growing at a rapid pace and now need to hire more staff, purchase another building, complete additional repairs, or even purchase more supplies. Time is ticking, and orders are piling up. The phone is ringing off the hook and your calendar is booked to capacity. It should be a business owner's dream! However, you've run into a roadblock, you are running out of money, and you need help fast! What do you do now? You are working around the clock to keep your clients at bay while you search for help. You need working capital to skyrocket your business to the next level. You are being asked to supply your profit and loss statement as well as your balance statement. However, you have not had a chance to look at your financials, or even hire a professional to take on this task for you. In the text below, we will discuss not only the importance of your business finances but how your business can continue to thrive in times of uncertainty and how you can finally begin to work on your business and not in your business.

Applying For a Business Loan

One of the most important financial statements your small business has is a profit and loss statement. As a start-up, your P&L statement is critical for many reasons, but it can also be used to assist you in getting the loan you need to finance your business. It gives lenders or investors a clear summary of your company and what they can expect from you. When applying for a small business loan, your P&L statement will contain important information like your company's projections. As lenders and investors see all small businesses as higher-risk investments, it is up to you to convince them that your business is worthy of lending. Proving your business's sustainability is key to getting accepted for a loan. Besides exceptional credit and your business plan, your P&L statement is one of the most important requirements for business loans. Another statement that is vital to your business is your balance sheet. The balance sheet shows a snapshot of your business assets and liabilities at any given time. This information is more valuable when the balance sheets for several consecutive periods are grouped so that trends in the different line items can be viewed. Lenders can look at your business assets in comparison to your current liabilities to determine if you would be able to pay off a loan. A lender or investor will also compare the total amount of debt to the total amount of equity listed on the balance sheet, to see if the resulting debt-to-equity ratio reveals a critically high level of borrowing. This information will reveal if the newly acquired debt will result in bad debt for the business. Investors also like to examine the amount of cash on the balance sheet to see if there is enough available to pay them a share. In short, the purpose of the balance sheet is to reveal the financial status of an organization, but lenders, investors, or creditors may focus on different information within the statement, depending on their own needs.

5 tips that will assist you with making sure that you are ready for funding:

1. **Familiarize Yourself with Helpful Tools**

Creating a P&L statement is far from simple. That's why you should take advantage of all available tools and resources to make yours top-notch. To make things easy, invest in cloud accounting software like QuickBooks. This guarantees your data is always up to date and makes it easy to input information from extra reports and reduces any hassle over maintenance data entry or other challenges.

2. **Get Clear About Your Goals**

Not knowing what your business income and expenses are at any given time can really hurt you. A P&L statement will not only assist you in recognizing the health of your business, but the lender will also be able to see how well or poorly your business is doing. You will be able to set goals, comparing your figures to a certain month, quarter, or year. You will be able to show how your business is advancing by showing the various time frames that you can use to prove your case. You want to be able to explain why and how your business has been profitable in the past, as well as explain any declines in your business if the question is raised.

3. **Acknowledge What Your P&L Statement Can do For You**

Your P&L statement should summarize your profit and losses as a business within an assigned time. It should cover any revenue you've incurred, losses made, or expenditure on goods. The statement should also provide a synopsis of what money you currently have as a business to be used on debts, salary, or to fund growth. What it will not do is tell you if you have enough money to pay bills.

4. Look into the Future

Any small business loan provider will want to see your financial estimates. They need to know what you forecast as far as any profits and losses, and how you plan to get from point A to point B. Be sure to project your numbers for at least one year into your business. If you can, try to shoot for three-year predictions as that will give lenders a better look at where your business is going. Make sure to set yourself clear monthly projections so that you convince a lender you're a good investment.

5. **Review and Refine**

Each month make it a priority to review your P&L statement and balance sheet. If you can review these statements on a weekly basis, that would be even better. If possible, connect with an accountant who can do this for you. Business is busy, but an accountant can help you meet your projections without adding to the hassle of day-to-day life. Your focus should be working on your business, not in your business. You want to keep an eye out for increased sales with declining profits, stagnant sales numbers, and large overhead expenses. Getting a business loan shouldn't be overwhelming and neither should preparation of a profit and loss statement.

Filing My Taxes

There are tax deadlines that must be met for small business owner, . You will need to know what your gross income and expenses are for the year before filing any required tax returns. If you do not file your tax return by your tax due date and you have a tax liability due to the IRS, you will be required to pay a late filing penalty, which will include interest. Before filing your taxes, it is good practice to provide your tax professional with your financial statements. You need good records to prepare your tax returns. These records must support the income, expenses, and credits you report. Generally, these are the same records you use to monitor your business and prepare your financial statement.

Recordkeeping

Per the IRS, you may choose any recordkeeping system that fits your business, but it must clearly show your income and expenses. You can choose to track your income and expenses with a simple journal, ledger or opt into using electronic accounting software. You want to ensure that you are keeping track of any supporting documents that you have as well. These documents should support the entries that are put on your tax return. Your supporting documents could include any W2's, 1099's receipts, invoices, or canceled checks for example. Your supporting documents may be needed to substantiate your purchase. It is vital that your supporting documents list the payee, amount paid, proof of payment, the date of transaction, and a description of the service. In short, anything that is placed on your tax return or into your ledger needs to have a supporting document proving where the income and expenses came from. If chosen for an audit, you will need to prove that your expenses are both ordinary and necessary to your business. It is good practice to get in a habit of capturing every single transaction that occurs in your business. When it comes to your business, you will want to create a paper trail, any business activity needs to be documented. You must keep your business records available at all times for inspection by the IRS. If the IRS examines any of your tax returns, you may be asked to explain the items reported. A complete set of records will help speed up the examination process.

Commingling Funds

As a business owner, you must keep your business and personal funds separate. You want to have a separate business bank account that only includes business income and expenses. Personal expenses are not eligible business expenses deductible against taxable income. Commingling your books or bank account is one of the most common ways that a business can receive an audit. In the event of an audit, you want clear financials that prove all your business income and expenses. Remember that the name of the game is to keep clear, clean financial records. Commingling of funds or assets is a legal breach of trust and makes it hard to determine which funds or assets belong to the company and which are personal. Commingling funds can open your business up to fraud allegations that you do not want to encounter. Even worse, when you mix business and personal expenses in the same bank and credit card accounts, you run the risk of losing legitimate tax deductions. To deduct items on your taxes, you need to be able to support those expenses and prove they're deductible to your business.

Paying Yourself as a Business Owner

Depending on which entity you choose when creating your business will determine how you will pay yourself. If you choose a limited liability company (LLC) sole proprietorship or partnership, then you will be paying yourself directly from your business bank account by taking distributions, transferring funds directly to your personal account, or writing yourself a check from your business bank account. You will want to make sure that these distributions are notated as owners draw. Depending on your partnership agreement, you may be eligible for guaranteed payments. On the other hand, if you elected S or C Corp status, you are now considered an employee of your business and you will be paying yourself a reasonable salary. You will want to research how much other business owners make in your field to determine your reasonable salary. It is important to note that corporations must pay themselves a salary first before taking any distributions from the business. It is important to note that if your business is taxed as a partnership or corporation you will have two tax returns to file, one business tax return, and one personal tax return. Your business tax return must be filed before your personal tax return. You must have all partner and shareholder pertinent information available before filing your business tax return. The tax-filing due date for your business if elected to be taxed as an S-Corp or partnership is on March 15th and the tax-filing due date for a C-corps is on April 15th. Now that you know how to pay yourself from your business appropriately, next we will discuss recordkeeping and why this is imperative to your business.

Is it necessary to keep records of my business activity?

To keep it simple, everyone who owns and operates a business must keep accurate records. Having good records will help you monitor the health of your business, prepare your financial statements, recognize sources of your income, keep track of your expenses, keep track of your property basis, and prepare accurate tax returns. Good records will also allow you to justify the items on your tax return. You will be able to see the fluctuations in your business income and expenses. You will likely forget what a certain expense was for by the time you need to file your taxes, and with good records, everything will already be documented for you. There will be times when you will need to receive funds from a lender, and you need to provide your financial statements in order to begin the process. The last thing you want to do is to be stuck without these statements which can be detrimental to your business. Accurate records can help you to prevent fraud. Having an overview of your business cash flow can allow you to understand how much cash is coming in and out of your business and produce an accurate financial statement for accounting and auditing purposes. Good recordkeeping practices are essential because it helps your business comply with various laws. Business owners should establish good accounting systems to drive good recordkeeping practices and retrieve or file records easily.

Next Steps

As a business owner, you are faced with ensuring that your business stays afloat. The day-to-day activities of running your business, providing awesome customer service, marketing, processing payroll, and keeping up with your employees can be quite a bit. I am sure that you want your business to be around for decades, and some of you may want to leave your business to your family. The last thing that you want is to be stuck worrying about proper financials. Maintaining accurate books can seem like a burden when you are trying to grow your business. However, if you want to strategize for long-term growth, your books must be in order. Not having good books can very well make or break your business. Importantly, it is a requirement per the IRS. The reason that you got into business was to make a profit, right? If you do not have your books in order, then how do you know where your business stands? By looking at your numbers you can implement business decisions and plans to push your business in the correct direction. Knowing what your available cash in hand is important for running your business and accurate bookkeeping can help you keep track of it at any given time. Business owners wear many hats, but it is very hard to grow your business and see exponential growth in your business by trying to do everything alone. I know your business is your baby, and you want to ensure that you have trustworthy individuals apart of your team who share your same vision. However, there comes a time in business when the pressure gets overwhelming and you need to hire more staff, your business may not be able to hold your clients, and or inventory in the same space anymore. You also will get to a place where business is doing so well, but you cannot tell anyone exactly how well, or how much you've increased. You can feel and see the growth, but you have not tracked your numbers. If you want to go fast go alone, if you want to go far go with others. You can go fast alone, but if you want to go far and create a staple in your community or in the world then you will need to hire a team. You will want to work on your business and not in your business. You will want to walk into true entrepreneurship. You will want to pass the torch and put SOPs (Standard Operating Procedures) in place that will let your staff know exactly how you need the job done. You do not want to be the business owner who has their hand in every single pot. You will have a very hard time reaching the level of success that you foresee carrying on this way. This is a sure sign that you need help. You need someone to partner with you to help oversee your business. You need someone to keep another eye on your numbers. You or your staff may not have the time, knowledge, expertise, or capacity to perform recordkeeping tasks timely and accurately. Outsourcing is a good way to get work done professionally and at an affordable cost. Focus on what you are good at and outsource the rest. Not good at accounting and recordkeeping? Don't know where to start? Get someone to do it instead. Use your time and energy wisely by concentrating on business activities that can help you drive productivity and profitability better. No use spending hours trying to figure out how to process your records when you can easily hire someone to do it professionally at a fraction of the cost. Now that we have gone through the importance of recordkeeping and provided you with recommendations on how to do so, we hope that you will stay vigilant and ensure that your records are properly maintained and retained!

Life Advice-Control Your Business

As you continue your journey of entrepreneurship, you should set boundaries early on for your business hours and how a potential client will contact you. It is a very good idea to set up a calendar like Acuity Scheduling or Calendly especially if you are working virtually. You will want to interview your clients by having a discovery call to ensure that you are both a good fit for one another. Controlling how your potential clients contact you will allow you to stay organized, prepare for your potential meetings and relieve stress and anxiety. You will be able to close your schedule as you see fit to run errands or manage your personal affairs. There is nothing worse than your potential clients contacting you in the wee hours of the morning and you responding or feeling as if you need to just so you won't lose a potential client. Business hours are set in place for a reason, and you need to make that clear from the beginning. We cannot go to a brick-and-mortar business that's closed and demand service, this should be the same mindset if you are running a virtual business.

ABOUT

Tax Strategist Patrice Jones founded Patrice Jones & Associates in 2020 as an online boutique providing a full range of tax and accounting services, including tax preparation, tax planning, bookkeeping, virtual CFO services, and business formation. She also assists clients with lowering their tax liability and staying IRS compliant.

With 7 years of industry experience, Patrice advises clients on past and current tax matters and offers tax law guidance to ensure their understanding of projected future returns. She devotes ample time to each client, ensuring every concern is addressed during each consultation.

Patrice believes the right mindset is crucial for personal growth and progress in life. She stresses the importance of surrounding oneself with successful individuals and maintaining persistence in all our endeavors.

Born and raised in Milwaukee, WI, Patrice earned an Applied Science Degree from Bryant & Stratton College in 2005 and is affiliated with the National Association of Tax Professionals. She holds a Fast Forward Academy Certificate of Completion from the IRS Annual Filing Season Program, is authorized to provide E-File services, and aspires to become an Enrolled Agent.

SHAKEEMAH MURRAY

As a business owner investing in short-term rental properties, it is imperative to plan and create a tax plan before the year is over. Tax planning is a proactive approach to running a successful business and involves evaluating your financial situation and making strategic decisions to minimize your tax liability while remaining complaint with tax laws.

Creating a tax plan, you can make certain that you are taking advantage of all available deductions and credits, optimizing your tax savings, and avoiding any potential penalties. Additionally, as a business owner with shorter-term rental properties, you may have unique tax considerations, such as the need to collect and remit occupancy taxes, which should be considered in your tax plan, creating a tax plan helps you manage your tax burden more effectively and reduce your overall business expenses.

What is a Short-term Rental Property?

Short term rental properties have become an increasingly popular opportunity to help you reduce your tax bill, earn extra income, and build a legacy for yourself. Short-term rentals give travelers an option to stay at your property versus staying at a traditional hotel. You can travel with your children or in groups. Short-term rental properties can offer several benefits over traditional hotels such as more space and privacy, the ability to cook meals, and often a lower cost per night.

Short-term rental property is a property that is rented out on a temporary basis, typically for less than 30 days. So, if you have properties such as apartments, condominiums, houses, and even rooms within a larger property you can rent it out.

Guests book through online platforms such as Airbnb, VRBO, or HomeAway, which will allow you the business owner to list your property and connect with potential renters. These platforms provide a convenient and easy-to-use booking system for you (owner) and renters.

Short-term rentals can potentially be a lucrative source of income for you. When you rent out your property on a short-term basis, you could earn rental income that can help cover the mortgage payments or other expenses. It's important to understand the specific regulations and tax implications in your area.

Short-term rental properties can be used for both personal and business purposes, and the key difference between the two lies in the intention behind the rental activity.

Personal use of a short-term rental property typically involves you renting out your property for a short period of time to individuals or groups for personal reasons as I briefly describe before. What this looks like is when individuals, friends or family go on vacations they look to Airbnb for private homes and listing spare bedrooms.

Business property for commercial purposes. This could look like using the property as a vacation rental business, where you as the owner rents out multiple properties to travelers for profit, or as corporate housing for business travelers. The primary motive for business use is usually to generate income from the property as a source of revenue.

Investing in short-term rentals

How can you help me with my tax goals?

In order to effectively create a tax strategy and plan, understand that when you file your tax returns every year, you are reporting the results of your activities from the previous year.

Most real estate investors are not taking a proactive approach to tax strategy and planning because they are not taking the right actions throughout the year some are just not aware of what they don't know because there is not a lot of information out here and it is challenging to understand.

One of the most important things to keep in mind during the year when renting out a property on a short-term basis is that all income earned from the rental must be reported to the IRS. Whether you are using Airbnb or renting out your property on your own, it's essential to accurately report your income to avoid any potential penalties or legal issues down the line.

What exactly counts as rental income? In short, any money you receive from renting out your property on a short-term basis is considered rental income. This includes not only the rental fee itself, but also any additional fees charged by the platform you're using, such as cleaning fees or service charges.

It's important to keep accurate records of all income earned from your short-term rental. This means keeping track of all payments received, whether through cash, check, or electronic transfer. You should also keep any receipts or invoices related to the rental, such as receipts for cleaning or maintenance services.

Reporting your rental income to the IRS is typically done on your annual tax return. If you earn more than $600 in rental income each year, the platform you're using may issue you a Form 1099-K, which will report the total amount of income earned through the platform.

If you are renting out your property on your own, you'll need to report your rental income on Schedule E of your tax return. This form is for reporting rental income and expenses. On this form, you'll report the total amount of rental income earned during the year, as well as any expenses related to the rental, such as cleaning fees or repairs.

In summary, reporting all income earned from short-term rentals is essential to maintaining compliance with the IRS and local regulations. Keep accurate records of all income and expenses related to your rental, report all rental income on your tax return, and consider working with a tax professional to ensure you're meeting all of your tax obligations.

What does tax planning & tax preparation look like?

Let's discuss what tax planning and preparation looks like.

1. Gather financial information: The first step in tax preparation is to gather all relevant financial information, such as income and expense records for the year. For

short-term rental owners, this might include rental income, expenses related to managing the property, and any taxes or fees paid to local governments.

2. Evaluate tax liability: Once you have all your financial information, you can evaluate your tax liability. This involves estimating how much tax you will owe based on your income and deductions. For short-term rental owners, you may also need to consider any occupancy taxes or other taxes owed to local governments.
3. Identify deductions and credits: The next step is to identify any deductions or credits that can be

used to lower your tax liability. For short-term rental owners, common deductions might include expenses related to maintaining and repairing the property, property management fees, and advertising expenses.

4. Develop a tax plan: Based on your evaluation of tax liability and available deductions and credits, you can develop a tax plan to optimize your tax savings. This might involve adjusting your business expenses or taking advantage of tax credits and deductions of which, you were previously unaware.
5. File taxes: Once you have developed a tax plan, you can file

your taxes using the appropriate forms and schedules. For short-term rental owners, this might include forms such as Schedule E (Supplemental Income and Loss) and Form 1065 (U.S. Return of Partnership Income) if you operate your rental property as a partnership.

6. Review and adjust: Finally, it is important to review your tax return after filing and make any necessary adjustments for the future. This might involve revising your tax plan or making changes to your business practices to optimize your tax savings in the coming year.

Tax Considerations for Short-term Rentals

Here are some key considerations to keep in mind:

1. Report all income: any income you receive from your short-term rentals is taxable and must be reported to the IRS. This includes both the rental income and any fees charged by the platform you're using. Keep accurate records of all income received and expenses related to the rental.
2. Deduct eligible expenses: you can deduct certain expenses related to your short-term rental, such as cleaning fees, repairs, and utilities. You may also be able to

deduct mortgage interest, property taxes, and depreciation if the rental property is also your primary residence. Keep in mind that you can only deduct expenses that are directly related to the rental property, not personal expenses.

3. Determine your tax status: Depending on how much you make from your short-term rental; you may be considered a small business owner or self-employed. This will affect how you report your income and expenses, as well as the deductions you're eligible for.
4. Understand local regulations: Some cities and states have

specific regulations regarding short-term rentals, such as licensing requirements or occupancy taxes. Be sure to research AND Comply with any local regulations that apply to you.

5. Consider working with a tax professional: If you're unsure about how to report your short-term rental income or which deductions your eligible for, consider working with a tax professional. They can help you navigate the tax code and ensure your reporting everything correctly.

Importance of "Placed into Service"

The term placed in service means the time that property is first placed by the taxpayer in a condition or state of readiness and availability for a specifically assigned function, whether for use in a trade or business, to produce income, in a tax-exempt activity, or in a personal activity.

Generally, your rental is ready for use when the city or locality of your rental property will issue a Certificate of Occupancy. The rental property is considered available for use once it's advertised for rent. The date placed into service is an important tax-related concept for short-term rental property owners because it determines the beginning of the property's depreciation.

Depreciation is a tax deduction that allows property owner to recover the cost of the property over a specified period of time typically 27.5 years for residential rental properties. So, it is important to accurately establish this date because it determines when depreciation can begin and how much can be deducted each year.

If the date placed into services is incorrectly established, it can result in a reduced tax deduction for depreciation or a disallowed deduction altogether. For example, if a rental property owner purchases a property and it needs severe renovations before its ready to rent. Any renovation cost incurred before you place the property in service must be cap claims depreciation for a property that has not yet been placed into service, the IRS may disallow the deduction, resulting in additional taxes owed.

Therefore, it is important for short-term rental property owner to accurately establish the date placed into service on day one to ensure that they can claim the appropriate amount of depreciation and maximize their tax deductions while remaining in compliance with tax laws.

Difference between Capital Improvements vs. Repairs and maintenance expense

What can I do differently to improve my tax situation and tax plan?

Understanding the difference between Capital improvements vs. Repairs and maintenance expense to improve your tax situation when it comes to short-term rental properties.

Capital improvements are expenses incurred to improve the value of a property or extend its useful life. These expenses are generally considered as long-term investments and can be depreciated over time.

Examples of capital improvements in a short-term rental property might include adding a swimming pool, renovating the kitchen or bathrooms, or installing new flooring. Repairs and maintenance expenses, on the other hand, are expenses incurred to keep the property in good working order. These expenses are generally considered to be short-term expenses and are not intended to extend the useful life of the property. Examples of repairs and maintenance expenses for a short-term rental property might include fixing a leaky faucet, repairing a damaged window, or replacing a faulty appliance.

It's important to distinguish between capital improvements and repairs and maintenance expenses for a short-term rental property because they are treated differently for tax purposes. Capital improvements can be depreciated over time, whereas repairs and maintenance expenses are typically expensed in the year in which they are incurred.

Additionally, capital improvements can increase the basis of the property, which can reduce the amount of taxable gain when the property is eventually sold. Repairs and maintenance expenses, on the other hand, do not increase the basis of the property and do not have any impact on the eventual taxable gain.

What other tax savings should I try to do this year?

What is the Augusta Rule?

Take advantage of, The Augusta Rule, "14-day Rule" known as IRS Section 280A, allows homeowners to rent out their home residence to their S-Corp, partnerships, C corps, and Limited Liability Co business for up to 14 days per year without needing to report the rental income on their individual tax return. Let me elaborate, you could rent out your home to your business if you live in the United States. It will work if Both your business and you as the business owner or shareholder's personal taxes simply by allowing the business to deduct the expenses of renting your personal residence for business purposes. Both your business and You don't have to report the income on your personal tax return.

The Augusta rule has history behind the name so back in the 1970s, The Augusta rule IRS exemption was lobbied by the people of residents in Augusta Georgia. Each year, the Masters golf tournaments were held in the Augusta National Golf Club, and residents of the city wanted to rent their homes to attendees of the tournament without becoming a rental business. So, by them coming together they succeeded and Section 280A was added to the tax code and now people all over the US can participate in the Augusta Rule.

",,,if a dwelling unit is used during the taxable year by the taxpayer as a residence and such dwelling unit is actually rented for less than 15 days during the taxable year, then.. the income derived from such use for the taxable year shall not be included in gross income..."

However, if you rent out your vacation home for more than 14 days during the year, you must report all rental income received on your tax return, and you can only deduct expenses related to the rental to the extent of the rental income received. If you use the property for personal use for more than 14 days or more than 10% of the total days it was rented out during the year, you may not be able to deduct all the rental expenses.

It's important to understand that the Augusta Rule only applies to rental properties that are considered primary residence, vacation home, not investment properties. For more information on the Augusta Rule visit, https://www.irs.gov/taxtopics/tc415

Anything else I can do to reduce my tax bill and improve my tax return?

What are Passive Activity Limits and Passive Losses?

You can reduce your tax bill by understanding Passive activity refers to any investment or business activity in which the investor does not materially participate in the operation or management of the activity. This includes activities such as rental real estate and limited partnerships.

The IRS defines material participation as regular, continuous, and substantial involvement in the operation or management of the activity. If an investor does not meet this standard, the activity is considered passive.

Passive activities can generate income or losses, but they are subject to different tax rules than active activities. Passive activity income is generally taxable, but passive losses may only be deductible to the extent of passive income generated during the same tax year. Any excess losses can be carried forward to future tax years to offset future passive income or gains.

Passive Losses occur when the expenses incurred to generate passive activities income exceed the income generated by the activity. For example, if you own a rental property that generates $10,000 of rental income but incurs $15,000 in expenses, you will have a passive loss of $5,000,. Passive losses can only be deducted up to the amount of passive income you have, and any excess limit.

To take losses against your ordinary income, you must demonstrate active participation in the activity. The tax treatment of passive activities is intended to prevent taxpayers from using passive losses to offset income from other sources, such as wages or salaries,

For more information visit https://www.irs.gov/pub/irs-pdf/p527.pdf

In conclusion, tax planning is a crucial element for short term rental property investors who want to maximize their profits and minimize their tax liabilities. By implementing effective tax planning strategies, property owners/investors can reduce their taxable income, take advantage of deductions and credits, proper record keeping, tracking expenses and income, and avoid penalties and interest charges. Hiring a qualified tax professional, Enrolled agent, or CPA are key to being a successful Rental property investor. Ultimately, by making tax planning a priority, short term rental property owners can ensure that they are operating their business in the most financially efficient and profitable manner possible.

ABOUT

Shakeemah Murray is a seasoned financial banking professional turned tax strategist and Tax & Business Strategy Accounting firm owner of Assured Accounting and Associates with over 20 years of experience in the financial services industry. She helps business and rental owners increase cashflow minimize taxes and leave a legacy.

Shakeemah began her professional career as a Financial Banker at a large bank after earning her degree in Business Administration with specialization in accounting. She rose through the ranks and became a highly regarded Bank Officer Executive within the company, thanks to her unique expertise in financial analysis, financial planning, business planning, strategy, and risk management. She brings this experience as a Tax Strategist.

After two decades of working in the financial services industry, A short time in Healthcare Pharmaceutical and other business endeavors, Life happened, Shakeemah realized that she was worth living a life she loved on her terms beyond motherhood, with a passion for financial tax planning and Serving Clients. She decided to further her education in order to navigate complex tax laws, & regulations studying for her Enrolled Agent Examination.

Prior to her relocation to NYS from NJ, Shakeemah was an active member in a number of professional organizations and communities including the New

Jersey Society of Certified Public Accountants (NJSCPA), National Association of Black Accountants (NABA), (NAWBO) National Association of Women Business Owners, Shakeemah consistently helps within her community, and have given her time and effort to the YMCA NJ, Habitat for Humanity. She volunteered in a religious organization called S.A.F.E (sisters acquiring female etiquette) an organization for girls aged 5 thru 18.

Outside of work, Shakeemah enjoys spending time with her 6 children, family, traveling, and Quiet time for reading or gardening. She is in the works for launching a Podcast focused on Self-Worth and Net Worth called She's Building Wealth.

As a business owner, you have enough to figure out right? There are meetings to attend, people to hire, people to fire, projects to complete, marketing, budgeting, and that's all before lunch. Whew, I am exhausted already just thinking about it, aren't you? After all that and more, you also must be aware of tax implications and properly plan for your taxes. It's what most business owners dread. So often my clients come to me and feel overwhelmed with even the thought of having to plan for their taxes each year. I just love when they come into my office and leave with a sense of relief. The weight of it all has been lifted from their shoulders. I'm sure just like many of my amazing clients, you are in the same boat. Tax planning is probably not the part of your business that gets much attention. You probably find yourself asking what does tax planning even look like? Where do I even start? Lucky for you, you're in the right place at exactly the right time. We'll discuss the following to get you started on the right path so that you can become a tax planning superhero for your business. We'll discuss choosing how your business wants to be taxed; the pros and cons of all the business structures so that you can choose which structure is best beneficial for you and your business; outlining what the tax preparation process looks like for your business to have an effective tax plan at year end; properly planning for your tax bill throughout the year; recordkeeping requirements; and eligible deductions and credits to assist in lowering your tax liability. By the end of this chapter, you will be able to identify if you should maintain your current tax election or change it; how to properly plan for taxes; and the process for keeping good records to avoid a tax adjustment as a result of an audit.

Ready, Set, Go! Choosing How You Want to Be Taxed.

By now, I'm sure you've seen floating around on social media the post that says, "Go and get an LLC. Once you have an LLC, go, and get an EIN number. Once you have an EIN number, go, and open a business bank account-that's how you start your business." Every time I see it, I always laugh because it is so misinforming and it's leaving out the most important step. I know, you've started your business already and probably have your LLC and EIN number. Now you are thinking I'm all set. But did you choose how you want your business to be taxed when you went through that process? As just an LLC you're taxed the same as a sole proprietor and that tax rate is 15.3 percent. 12.4 percent is paid to Social Security and 2.9 percent is paid to Medicare. During the process of applying for your EIN number, the application will ask you how you want to be taxed. This step in the process will determine how much tax your business pays at year end. You can choose to be taxed as an LLC, a C-Corporation, an S-Corporation, or as a partnership. All four tax elections have different ways and rules of taxation. This is where you want to choose the tax election that's going to be the most beneficial for you. Let's dive deeper into each tax election and get a better understanding of how they work, and which one will be most applicable and beneficial for your business.

Is an LLC What's Best for Me?

What is an LLC? An LLC is a limited liability company that lets you take advantage of the benefits of both the corporation and partnership business structures. The profits and losses get passed through to your personal income without facing corporate tax rates. However, members of an LLC are considered self-employed and must pay the self-employment tax contributions towards Medicare and Social Security. The benefits of being taxed as an LLC can be good for medium or higher risk business owners with significant personal assets they want to protect and owners who want to pay a lower tax rate than they would pay if they elected to be a corporation. The drawback is that 15.3 percent can add up quickly, and you can face a large tax bill if you don't properly plan for the tax liability by year end.

The most important factor to remember when you're taxed as an LLC is that taxes are a pay-as-you-go system. This means that you need to pay most of your taxes during the year, as you receive income. The best option for an LLC would be to make quarterly estimated tax payments. Planning to make quarterly estimated tax payments will reduce your tax liability at the end of the year and if you plan correctly it could also generate a refund. Each state is different so you will want to research your specific states department of revenue website to determine what their tax rate is and make your quarterly payments to them as well. Federal quarterly estimated tax payments are due 4 times per year. Those due dates are April 15th, June 15th, September 15th, and January 15th. If these due dates fall on a Saturday, Sunday or legal holiday, the quarterly payment is due the next business day.

Now-you're probably asking as an LLC how do I know how much to pay each quarter? No worries-lets break it down. On irs.gov you can find form 1040-ES. You will want to use this worksheet to compute what your taxable income for the year will be. You can use your prior year's tax return as a starting point for the first quarter and complete a new form to readjust accordingly throughout the year up or down as needed. You'll complete the form for each quarter to calculate your estimated tax payment. The worksheet will consider your standard deduction, any qualified business deductions, as well as any refundable credits for which you may qualify. Once you have the worksheet completed you can make your estimated payment.

There are many options for sending in the estimated payment. You can either send the payment in with form 1040-ES or by going to irs.gov/payments. Once you're on their website you'll see the options to make the payment. You can make a payment without creating an account, but I highly suggest you create an account so that you can keep the history of the payments made and access it when needed. The beauty in this process is that if you overpay your estimated taxes, it's refunded back to you when you file your tax return for that tax year. And on the other side, if you underpay, your liability upon filing will not be nearly as much as it would be if you didn't make any payments. By following the estimated tax plan steps for an LLC, you can avoid a huge bill at the end of the year. One thing you can be certain of is that the IRS will get their payment. It's just up to you how you want them to collect it. This is the best way to ensure you're properly planning for your taxes within your LLC. In most cases, by making quarterly estimated payments once you file your return and account for all of your business expenses you will be pleased at the outcome as expenses reduce the adjusted gross income-thereby reducing the amount of tax due.

There are many misconceptions being communicated on the pros and cons of choosing to remain taxed as an LLC. I want to inform you of those misconceptions. Have you ever heard someone say that you're supposed to take a loss on your business? Well, if you're always writing everything off on your personal tax return for your LLC, then how do you show your business made any money for the year. If you can't show your business made money, then it will be hard for you to do other investments or leverage the banks' capital. In order to do those things, you have to show that your business is profitable. By making those quarterly estimated payments is a great way to do that. By making quarterly estimated payments, you don't have to report as many expenses to get your tax bill down. Which in turn will report more income on the return without the tax penalties since you made quarterly estimated payments throughout the year. Making quarterly estimated payments allows you to keep a higher income which has several benefits. Let's say you want to purchase a home. Your LLC is reported on your personal tax return. Your income must be at least 25 percent of your loan approval amount. If you're always writing off everything on your tax return to reduce the tax liability instead of making quarterly estimated payments, your business doesn't show on paper that it can qualify for the loan you're looking for. The same thing applies if you want to get working capital or lines of credit. The misconceptions will make you believe that you must write everything off so that you don't take a loss, but you're losing out on the possibilities of investment properties, working capital, etc. Now that you know the more beneficial way, you're set up for success. Your tax bill is now reduced due to quarterly estimated payments, you're showing that your business made money, and you can leverage the banks' money to grow your business as a result. I'd say it's a win! As an LLC you now have the tools to properly plan for your taxes, you know how to reduce your tax bill at year end, and how it affects the tax return and leveraging capital.

Do I See Corporation in my Future?

A Corporation, often referred to as a C-Corp, is a legal entity that is separate from its owners. C-Corps can make a profit, be taxed, and can be held legally liable. Unlike an LLC, Corporations are taxed a flat rate of 28 percent which is an increase from the prior year in which the rate was 21 percent. C-Corps pay income tax on their profits. In some cases, corporate profits are taxed twice.

First when the company makes a profit, and again when dividends are paid to shareholders on their personal tax return. Corporations can be a good choice for medium or higher risk businesses and those that need to raise money. They are also a good tax election for businesses that plan to go public or eventually be sold.

As a business owner you've most likely had to make the decision as to what type of company you want to be. Or maybe you haven't and that's why you're here. Many entrepreneurs struggle to make the decision to become a corporation or an LLC. The owner or owners of the C-Corp are separate from the corporation. And due to that fact, the business can earn money, and they are taxed on such funds earned and only the corporation is held liable for any wrongdoings. Once you choose to be taxed as a C-Corp, the owner of the corporation becomes an employee and receives a salary. There are taxes paid by said employee from their withholdings. Entrepreneurs usually don't choose to be taxed as a C-Corp and such tax elections are much less common than LLC's and S-Corps.

There are many advantages to choosing the C-Corp tax election such as protection from personal liability and the ability to sell stocks and bonds, which makes it easier to raise capital. You can have an unlimited number of investors, and the lifespan of the company is indefinite. The disadvantages of choosing a C-Corp election is that the corporation incurs its expenses up front. They also must conform to a lot of regulations-hence why good recordkeeping is necessary, and they incur double taxation. Double taxation occurs as the C-Corp is taxed at their rate of 28 percent and once the profits are disbursed to the shareholders-they're taxed again on their personal tax return. What does that mean for you? That means that your C-Corp's profits are taxed on the C-Corps tax return and as a shareholder of the Company you pay taxes again on your personal tax return. Highway robbery, I know. C-Corps pay more tax than an LLC because it is treated as its own entity by the IRS. But no need to worry if this is your tax election. Let's dive into how you can properly plan and reduce that 28 percent tax you'll have to pay.

As a corporation, you must file tax Form 1120 each year by April 15th. If this date falls on a holiday or a Saturday, it's moved to April 18th. The difference between an LLC and a Corporation is that if the return is not filed on time by the due date, including extensions, there is a penalty of 5 percent of the unpaid tax for each month or part of a month that the return is late; not to exceed 25 percent of the unpaid taxes. This filing requirement must be met to avoid unnecessary tax implications for the corporation. We'll discuss several ways to reduce the tax and properly plan for C-Corps.

Since we know that the corporation gets hit with double taxation, some ways to reduce the corporation's flat taxes that are due is to have employee fringe benefits, deducting health insurance premiums paid on behalf of an owner-employee, and deducting other business expenses. There are savings on self-employment taxes, as corporate income is not subject to Social Security, Workers Compensation and Medicare taxes. The C-Corp should include fringe benefits such as medical insurance, life insurance, assistance with childcare, transportation reimbursements, employee meals and even tuition reimbursement. Accountable plans are also another great way to reduce taxes for the C-Corp. If the C-Corp has employees, they are likely reimbursing them for some of their expenses. This may include things like entertainment or even travel. Using an accountable plan allows you to reimburse employees for business expenses without reporting them as employee income. More employee income means more payroll taxes the C-Corp would have to pay. Therefore, by using an accountable plan you're reducing the employee income, and reporting less employers' wages paid, which in turn generates less employers' taxes to be paid. Savings on top of Savings! Hiring your family or spouse in the C-Corp can also help to reduce taxes and create a savings for the corporation. If your children or your spouse help with the business or assist with day-to-day operations, putting them on payroll for their work can save on taxes for the corporation. Children can work tax free, assuming you follow the IRS income tax thresholds. And to take it a step further you can open your children a ROTH IRA account with their income.

A crucial tax planning tip for C-Corps is to manage the timing of their income and expenses. A good strategy is to accelerate expenses and defer income. You can slow your income down by delaying sending invoices or making the due date for invoices to be the following year instead of the 4th quarter of the year. For example, if you perform a service in November, instead of invoicing the customer with a due date of December, make the due date January. This strategy doesn't count the income on that invoice in the tax year in which the service was performed but counts it for the following tax year. Keep your expenses the same during this strategy thereby decreasing your taxable income for the year. On the other hand, it might make more sense to accelerate income into the current year, especially if you think tax rates will increase in the near future. In this case, you can send your invoice and try to collect payment from the customer in the current year, so more income will be taxed at the current year's tax rate. Ideal timing of income and expenses depends on the C-Corps future outlook. If the C-Corp expects significantly higher personal income the following tax year, it can save on taxes to get the income during the current tax year.

Now, let's talk depreciation. It is a benefit used for business owners. Depreciation allows the business to record an assets loss in value as an expense. This expense helps to reduce taxable income and therefore decreases taxes due. Usually, depreciation has to be spread over years, however the federal law allows businesses to depreciate 100 percent of qualified property up to 1 million dollars the year it was acquired. This strategy is only true for property that was put into service after September 27, 2017, and before 2023. For property put into service in 2023 and beyond, the deduction drops to 80 percent of the qualified property. This first-year bonus depreciation means a business can deduct from income the entire purchase price of some types of property such as computers, software, equipment, machinery, furniture, vehicles, and building improvements. Yes, you're thinking is correct-you've just unlocked the cheat code!

Tax credits can also have a huge impact on reducing a C-Corps tax bill as well. Unlike deductions which reduce the business' taxable income, credits directly reduce the amount of tax owed. A tax saving credit is the Work Opportunity Tax Credit. The WOTC is designed to help employers hire and retain individuals from certain target groups that have consistently faced significant barriers to employment. This includes members of families receiving benefits under the temporary assistance for needy family's program, felons, veterans, and those from other target groups. The credit is worth up to $2,400 per eligible new hire. To be eligible for this tax saving credit, businesses must hire individuals who are a member of one of the target groups, complete Form 8850 and submit the form to a designated local state agency within 28 days from the new hire's start date. Once the state agency confirms the employee is eligible for the credit, the corporation can claim the credit on the next regularly filed tax return.

Another tax saving credit is the disabled access credit. This credit is designed to help business owners offset some of the costs associated with providing access for people with disabilities. The credit is worth up to 50 percent or up to $10,000 in eligible expenses, but you cannot claim the credit on the first $250 of qualifying expenses. To claim this tax saving credit, your business must have a revenue of 1 million dollars or less and no more than 30 full time employees. Eligible expenses that qualify for the credit are: modifying existing facilities to make them accessible for disabled individuals, offering braille, large print, and audio versions of materials, providing a sign language interpreter or reader for customers or employees, or purchasing adaptive equipment. By implementing these tax saving credits you are sure to reduce your tax bill at the end of the year and your shareholders will thank you!

Me and You Just Us Two or More-All about Partnerships

Are you in business with one or more people? Then you should be taxed as a partnership. Partnerships are the simplest structure for two or more people to own a business together. There are several types of partnerships. In a general partnership, all partners have unlimited liability, so the individual partners are jointly and separately responsible for the partnership's obligations. In a limited partnership a limited partner's liability is limited to their investment, provided they are not actively involved in the management of the firm. In a limited liability company (LLC), all partners have limited liability. When you're taxed as a partnership, the profits are passed through to the partners on a Schedule K1 and are reported on the partner's personal tax return. The income, deductions and credits flow through to each partner and there isn't any tax at the partnership level creating only one layer of taxation unlike the C-Corp-creating huge tax savings. Partnerships are a great tax election for businesses with multiple owners, professional groups such as attorneys, and groups who want to evaluate their business idea before forming a more formal business.

The beauty of partnerships is that the contributions to and distributions from the partnership can be made without any income tax consequences, therefore planning for taxes at year end is all the simpler. Partnerships don't have to calculate or pay any taxes at the partnership level. Within a partnership the partners share the expenses, and the net income is what gets carried to each partner according to their share percentage. Each partner then pays the taxes on the income according to their own specific tax rate for the income on their personal tax return. Even charitable contributions paid by the partnership pass through to each partner's personal return which reduces their tax liability. All partners are considered equal in the eyes of the IRS unless the partnership has a special agreement in place that outlines each partner's specific share of the business.

By recognizing it as such, it can allow a tax break when a new partner becomes a part of the company as the taxable assets in the partnership will decrease. Partnerships can allocate income and have the right to split ownership, income, and voting rights.

An LLC makes estimated tax payments a partnership does not. However, to properly plan for taxes as a partner in a partnership, if the partner is going to owe more than $1,000 at the end of the year then the partner would want to make quarterly estimated payments to lower their liability following the instructions discussed in the LLC section of this chapter. It can be considered a pro and a con to be taxed on the individual level in a partnership.

One of those reasons is because business taxes generally have a lower rate than individual taxes, but due to the pass-through income within a partnership, the partners may pay more individually than if the company was a different structure. Each partner is responsible for their self-employment tax on their share of the partnership income and any guaranteed payments they receive. That's the same 15.3 percent as in an LLC. Depending on the partner's share of the profits that tax liability could be very high. Partners are not employees unlike Corporations. Which means the partnership saves in having to pay their employer's share of payroll taxes. There are a variety of deductible expenses a partnership can include to reduce the partnership income that is split between the partners. Such expenses include startup expenses, operating and marketing costs, travel, meals and entertainment, rents paid, repairs and maintenance, taxes and licenses, retirement plans, and depreciating property and assets. Partners also can take the qualified business income deduction which allows the partners to deduct up to 20% of their portion of business income in addition to any other business deductions.

The planning and preparing of the partnership return has much more simplicity than Corporations. Partnerships file what is called an information return using Form 1065. The partnership must also prepare a

Schedule K1 and issue those schedules to each partner which outlines each partners distribution of the taxable profits and or losses of the business to then be passed through to each partner's personal tax return. Spouses who own a partnership can elect to be a qualified joint venture which means instead of filing the Form 1065 they would file two Schedule Cs on their personal tax return. There are certain tests to see if spouses can qualify to use this tax planning strategy. Both persons must materially participate and there cannot be any other owners in the partnership. Out of all the tax structures, partnerships are the easiest to manage, file, and are taxed at the individual level the same as an LLC. There isn't much that goes into tax planning for partnerships as the partnership doesn't pay the tax at the entity level. It is mostly up to each partner to properly plan by making quarterly estimated payments to ensure their liability is not over the top at the end of the year.

Saving My Favorite Structure for Last-Let's Talk S-Corps

I could be biased, but the S-Corporation is the best tax election since sliced bread. I personally made the switch and went from owing the IRS over 80K in federal taxes and owing the State 15K in taxes to owing 0.00 for both. I mean it's a complete win all around the board. What is an S-Corp? S-Corps are corporations that elect to pass the corporate income, losses, deductions, and credits through to their shareholders for federal tax purposes. Shareholders of S-Corporations report the flow-through of income and losses on their personal tax returns and are assessed taxes at their individual income tax rates. This allows S-

Corporations to avoid double taxation on the corporate income. Before you can elect to be classified as an S-Corp, you must meet a specific set of requirements as defined by the IRS. Primarily, it needs to be a domestic corporation in the US; the number of shareholders cannot exceed 100; shareholders can only consist of individuals, estates, and some trusts; cannot be a partnership or other corporation; and cannot issue more than one class of stock. You can also be an LLC but choose to be taxed as an S-Corp. To do so you would need to file Form 2553.

The advantages of choosing to be taxed as an S-Corp are endless. We'll start with a few. Unlike Corporations, there is no double taxation. S-Corps are pass through entities and don't have to pay federal or state taxes. When the net income passes through to the shareholders, the tax is much lower than other tax elections. This is because shareholders report the income they receive from the company as a salary as required by IRS rules. S-Corps must be placed on a reasonable salary. When shareholders place themselves on a salary, they're reducing the amount they pay in self-employment tax. S-Corps also have asset protection, meaning if you choose the S-Corp election, your personal assets are separated from your company's assets. This is ideal and important because as the owner of the S-Corp, if the business ever goes bankrupt or gets sued, your personal assets aren't at risk. We're going to also manifest that your business does not experience any bankruptcies.

As much as I am in favor of the S-Corp election there are some draw backs as well. There are ownership restrictions. There cannot be more than 100 shareholders in the corporation. There are also stock restrictions, and you can only hold one class of stock which limits the amount of capital you can raise as well as voting rights. There is also a higher level of IRS security as the IRS is very much aware of those who try to disguise their salaries as distributions to avoid paying the payroll taxes from the salary you must pay yourself. The payroll requirement states that the salary must be reasonable in nature and comparative to the industry you're in. The plus side is the same reasonable salary you pay yourself reduces the profits of the corporation. Any profits that remain are not subject to self-employment tax. As you pay yourself a salary, you also pay your share of payroll taxes; federal and state as applicable; unemployment insurance; workman's compensation insurance; and file the applicable quarterly reports. I know it sounds like you're paying more for other taxes, but here's the catch. The payroll taxes are an expense that can be written off on the S-Corp tax return, thereby reducing the amount of income passed through to the shareholders. If you own the S-Corp and are paying yourself too high of a salary, you could be overpaying in thousands of dollars on your S-Corp's payroll taxes. Of course, you need to pay yourself a reasonable compensation for the position you hold and the job you're performing, but you want to make sure you're not overpaying yourself to save on the payroll tax end of things.

Now the filing of the S-Corp return is due on the 15th of the third month of each year. One of the first things you're going to want to prepare are your financial statements. A good tax professional will ask for these statements to properly prepare your S-Corp tax return. Even if you're doing the return yourself, you want your financial statements handy to assist in the preparation of the return. Your financial statements should include your year-to-date profit and loss statement, cash flow statements, and your balance sheet. These financial statements will contain most of the information you need to complete the return. You'll also want to make sure that all Forms W2 and 1099 have been filed for all employees and contractors for the company. The due date for the information forms is January 31st of each tax year. Like the partnership the 1120-S is an information return as the S-Corp doesn't pay any taxes. The form is completed to report all income, losses, credits, and deductions.

Most S-Corp shareholders should be able to save additional payroll taxes by having their S-Corp pay for their family's health insurance coverage. If it is included as part of their wages and their spouse is not eligible for coverage under a subsidized health insurance plan, it's a great benefit for tax planning. While the premiums included as wages are taxable personally and subject to income tax withholding, the amount paid is deductible as a wage expense by the S-Corp and the premiums are exempt from employment taxes. What does that mean for the S-Corp? That means that the premium is considered self-employed health insurance and therefore is deductible on a shareholder's personal income tax return as well. Wow, right, such a huge tax savings.

Under current tax laws, employees can no longer deduct out-of-pocket business expenses on their personal returns. As a result, the only option for employees is to get reimbursed by the corporation creating a tax savings. These reimbursable expenses can include home office rent, car mileage, transportation costs, cell phones, internet plans and more.

Like Corporations, the S-Corp will need to set up an accountable plan, which is used for reimbursing workers for business expenses that are not counted as income. An accountable plan requires expenses to be substantiated for business purposes, where excess payments are returned within a reasonable time. It's important to note that personal use of these expenses must not be reimbursed by the S-Corp and submitting incorrect expenses can be a red flag with the IRS. When creating an accountable plan for this tax planning and saving purpose it's helpful to keep a shortlist of popular deductions and expenses for you and the team. There is also a SEP IRA an S-Corp can provide for retirement contributions up to 25 percent of an employee's compensation or $61,000 whichever is less. The contributions to an SEP can also generate tax savings for the S-Corp.

An S-Corp owned by either a single individual or a married couple and without any other employees can set up a solo 401K plan and defer up to $20,500 of income per individual from taxes. As an employee, the amount of the contribution made to a solo 401k plan will reduce the employers SEP IRA Contribution limit. Th is another tax savings. Choosing the S-Corp tax election under the SEP IRA strategy lets you defer paying taxes. Any income will be taxed when it's taken out of the contribution plan at your gradual rates. Keep in mind if you decide to contribute to a retirement plan, the time of the year can affect the tax savings. You want to make sure you contribute before the tax filing deadline to make the most of the tax savings.

An amazing benefit of the S-Corp is having an employee under your own roof. There is so much tax savings for hiring your children. In 2022, each child employed in the family S-Corp can earn up to $12,950 without paying any personal federal income taxes. This decreases the income taxes for the family. Even though the S-Corp will have to pay the payroll taxes on the wages, you'll still save and come out ahead overall. To use this tax saving strategy, your child will need to be at least 7 years of age and must be completing an actual job for the business. It's also important that you pay your child the same amount you would pay any other employee to complete the job you hired them for. All other miscellaneous procedures should be completed as well such as onboarding, filing of W2 etc. The business reports the child's wages with

Salaries and Wages on Form 1120S which reduces the income overall that passes through to the shareholders.

Another great tax planning tip for S-Corps is if you travel for business. You don't want to forget to reimburse yourself for travel expenses that were paid out of pocket. You just need to make sure you do it the right way by submitting an expense report and reimbursing yourself through the business account to create a deduction for the S-Corp. The business will report reimbursed travel expenses with other deductions on Form 1120S.

Now here is one of my favorites, renting your home to your business. If you plan to hold meetings in your home or use your home for any other business-related gatherings throughout the year, you can charge your business rent for that use. Paying yourself rent could result in big tax savings since the S-Corp can deduct the amount of rent and you'll have more personal income that will be free from income tax. The only drawbacks are that you can rent only 14 days or less of use during the year and you should keep a record of the purpose of the rental. The rent should also be in line with what similar spaces in the area would charge for that same amount of time and use. Your business will report the rental expenses as Rents on the Form 1120S.

You can also rack up a major tax savings with a heavy vehicle deduction, which is known as a Section 179 deduction especially if you have a home office. To qualify for this deduction, there are several requirements. The three main requirements are the vehicle can be new or used, but the vehicle must be new to you, the vehicle must be titled in the company's name, and the vehicle must be used at least 50 percent of the time for business. In the eyes of the IRS, a heavy vehicle is any vehicle with a gross vehicle weight rating of more than 6,000 pounds. This includes many SUV's, crossovers, and full-size pick-up trucks. If the vehicle you choose is an SUV, your deduction will be limited to $25,000, but others are only limited to $1,080,000. Having a home office helps reach the 50 percent use towards business miles. Anytime you leave your home to complete tasks for business, those miles count towards your business miles. You'll want to make sure you're keeping track of your business miles so you can show you've met the 50 percent requirement. In addition, the initial Section 179 deduction also qualifies for 50 percent depreciation bonus when you buy a new vehicle. For used vehicles you can also use the modified accelerated cost recovery system depreciation bonus over five years. This can cause major tax benefits as you deduct the expense which reduces the income shared in the S-Corp.

I've Made My Tax Election, What Next?

Whew, that was a lot of information, right? Hopefully by now you're fully knowledgeable on the different types of tax elections and can make an informed decision. Now that you've chosen how you want to be taxed, let's look at what you need to have in place to plan accordingly through the year to ensure you have the max amount of tax savings. The most important factor to remember with tax planning is regardless of which entity you choose you will want to ensure that you're knowledgeable on how each entity affects your tax planning strategy. If you're already in business and now you realize you haven't chosen the tax election that is most beneficial for your business, it's not too late. You can file Form 8832 and elect to be treated as a corporation. You can also use Form 2553 to elect to be taxed as an S-Corp as well.

As a business owner the burden of proof relies on you to prove that you are in business with the intent to make a profit and not a hobby. Due to the burden of proof relying on you, recordkeeping is necessary. Having accurate, organized records about your business's income, expenses, and deductions can be the deciding factor on if your business faces income, expense, or tax deductions in an audit. I've experienced this firsthand with my clients. There was an instance whereby a client who has an LLC and makes over 1 million dollars a year was audited. The IRS was proposing adjustments in the amount of a little over 13 thousand dollars. Because we had accurate records of their books, income, expenses, and deductions, I was able to save my client from an IRS adjustment of over 13K. What does that mean? That means that had we not had her records in place and couldn't prove the expenses that were in question, the 13K would have been added to my client's tax bill increasing it by that amount. There are also times when I go through a client's bank statements and find eligible ordinary and necessary business expenses that were not included on their return. Recently I reduced a client's tax bill down by 45 thousand dollars just by thoroughly going through their bank statements. As you plan for taxes throughout the year you want to make sure you're keeping all records, aware of all the deductions the business can take, and organizing those records for easy access if questioned to verify by the federal or state agencies.

The most accurate way to keep business records is to have business bank accounts. Ideally you want to have 3 accounts. One account for your payroll expenses including wages, taxes, and insurance. A second account for the salary you pay yourself and a third account or your operating account where the sales/income flows in and all expenses are taken out. This would be the best way to stay organized and everything is accessible by pulling your business bank statements. Do not co-mingle your business accounts with your personal accounts. There are instances where business owners use a personal account for expenses and deductions and the IRS doesn't include the expenses as ordinary and necessary to the operation of the business because they were used from a personal account. You want to make sure your business accounts are being used for what they are intended and that all personal transactions run through your personal bank account. By using this strategy, you have all your income and expenses in one place to easily manage and track your estimated taxes if you have to pay them. There are online systems that you can use that will synchronize your business bank accounts and categorize expenses for you. They will also give you a tax estimate to show you what your estimated tax liability will be at year end based on the income and expenses synchronized from the accounts. Keeping your business accounts in order will be key to your tax planning journey throughout the year.

What Strategy Works for Me?

As a business owner properly planning for taxes is often a struggle when you first start out. The struggle comes from a lack of understanding and knowledge relating to the topic. It takes a lot of reading, researching, and trial and error to get to the place you want to be within your business. Often you must adjust your tax planning strategy as your business grows and changes. Your business can go up or down depending on several factors and you want to make sure the tax election you choose is flexible with the growth of your business. For example, an S-Corp may not be the best tax election for an LLC that has less than 50K in annual sales. Remember, an S-Corp must place themselves on payroll, which means an added expense of payroll taxes for both the federal and state. Those payroll taxes may drain the business due to the sales being under 50K. Once the business writes off their business expenses and apply their standard deduction, they should be in the clear depending on if they qualify for any other refundable credits. In this example the company with less than 50K in annual sales would want to remain an LLC as that would be the best strategy for reducing their tax liability.

An LLC may not be the right tax election for a business that has a higher income profit, as the 15.3 percent of self-employment tax can get expensive as the LLC generates more revenue and not as many expenses. As the income grows, the LLC would phase out of the refundable credits that they previously qualified for due to income phase out limits. So how do you know which election is right for you? You just have to make an informed decision at the time-remember it can always be changed later. I've found that starting out initially as an LLC was best for me. I have children so I qualified for refundable credits and after I reported all of my expenses, I was getting a refund. However, as my business grew those tax bills grew as well and the refund disappeared. It was at that moment I had to make the transition to the best tax election for the business as the business changed. By changing my tax election and adjusting my tax planning strategy it was more beneficial for my business's success.

I properly planned for taxes the year prior to my conversion to an S-Corp. I placed myself on a reasonable salary, filed all the required quarterly payroll reports, and backdated my election to that tax year. I was able to take my 80K tax bill as an LLC down to 0.00 as an S-Corp. I placed my children on payroll as well so that I could deduct their wages as an expense. I set them up IRA accounts to use that as a deduction as well. I was also able to purchase a vehicle in my business name and use the Section 179 deduction. The annual retreat I hosted at my home each year for my employees and contractors; I was able to deduct as I rented my home to the business for the 3-day event. I separated my business bank accounts so that I was organized for all my records and had the appropriate financial statements to be able to complete the S-Corp tax return. Putting all these things in place in advance helped me save thousands on my tax bill the following tax year. I now qualified for all these deductions for the S-Corp which lowered the net income that passed through to my personal return. It also helped me show that the business was profitable which led to business funding and lines of credit from the bank where my business accounts were housed. I knew going into that tax year that I needed a new strategy to best plan for taxes at the end of the year. Being proactive worked best for me and I would suggest as you enter year after year, you start the year and be proactive as well by using the prior year to forecast where you'll end the current year and plan accordingly at month one.

For me, I was also motivated to properly plan for taxes because I knew there was no way I wanted to keep making quarterly estimated payments and ending the year with a huge tax bill. I knew that there was something that could be done, I just needed to properly plan and execute. By educating myself on all of the tax elections I was able to make an informed decision on which one was best suited for my business growth and business needs. I knew if I could educate my clients on tax planning clearly I can do it for myself. I was in my own way, and I had to place myself at the feet of someone else who was an expert at tax planning to further educate myself on my options. It started out as the hardest task I set out to do. I ran through all the pros and cons and when it boiled down to it, I knew that the decision had to be made for change. It felt good the first year knowing I was not going to have to pay an enormous amount on my tax bill and that money could stay within the business. By adding my children on to payroll and setting them up with health insurance and retirement accounts I now had access to deductions that I did not have before as an LLC. It was by far one of the best decisions I made within my business. With the help of a business coach, I was able to self-teach myself what needed to be done so that my business could continue to thrive. Not only thrive but show profitability. Yes, I was one of the people I mentioned that was writing every little thing off on my personal tax return to reduce my tax liability and get a refund. Keeping all my receipts, making charitable donations, deducting all of my mileage-reducing my income all at the same time. I found myself wanting to purchase a property and couldn't qualify for the loan because on paper my business was in the red. Imagine my surprise when I realized that it looks like my successful business doesn't make any money and now, I'm unable to leverage the banks money to fund my business. I 'm unable to get approvals for loans on personal and investment properties because I had a poor tax strategy. My tax strategy was not conducive to where I wanted to take the business. For me to grow in business I had to make a decision financially to create a better tax planning strategy.

Choosing the appropriate tax election for my business was life changing for my tax planning strategy. Now I can see what my business brings in, I have a salary for myself, I have a health and retirement account that I can deduct, I rent my property to myself each year for my annual retreat, placed my children on payroll, and reimburse myself for all business travel expenses. Trust me those add up. I had to change my mindset. I was the person who wanted to get a refund every year. Once I shifted my mindset from poverty to profitable, I was able to make the best tax planning decision for my business. I learned that a refund means I have less income. Getting a refund meant that I was low income. How can I be low income when my business brings in 6 figures a year? It was because I was writing off so many expenses bringing my income down to around 20K annually. The only benefit from writing everything off was that I received a refund for the refundable credits of my children. Writing everything off prevented me from growing and reaching the goals I set for myself personally and professionally. What I had planned for my life and my business-I could not sit in that mindset. There was no way that I could stay in the mindset of if I make more, I won't get a refund. My initial strategy was changing my mindset and understanding there is a better way. I cannot remain stuck in the low mindset I'd acquired. I had to think high energy attracts high paying clients. We've turned 6 figure years, to 6 figure months-so I knew there had to be a plan for taxes at year end. Now we all have to pay taxes, but the law states that we must only pay our fair share of those taxes. By choosing the correct tax election, you are reducing your tax and planning appropriately so that you are only paying your fair share. My mind was in my way until I realized I can do so much more for myself, my children, and my community just by changing my tax planning strategy.

Creating Your own Strategy for Tax Planning

As business owners we have so much we have to juggle. We've identified which tax election you should choose so by now you are on the right track. We have all the facts, pros, and cons, and now we just need to decide on how we change our tax liability. The footwork has already been done throughout this chapter. You have a foundation on where you need to start. Once you choose your tax election, it's time to outline what it will take to get to the results you desire to end the year with. As an LLC or partnership, you want to choose a strategy of properly planning for your estimated taxes. We must remember that partnerships are pass through entities and although the partnership doesn't pay any taxes, each partner pays the taxes as the income passes through to their personal tax return therefore setting up estimated payments will be ideal. It is ideal especially if the partners are taking guaranteed payments and or distributions. Use the available worksheet on IRS.gov to determine what your estimated tax will be. You can set calendar reminders 5 days before each due date to remind you to make your quarterly estimated payment. You can set up another business account solely for the purposes of adding income to it and deducting the quarterly estimated payment. By using your organized business accounts, you can properly forecast the income you have against your expenses to aid in determining the estimated payment for the quarter. Once you make all your payments and begin preparing your tax return, you will see how your strategy of planning throughout the year was beneficial for your business.

As an S-Corp you should choose the strategy of carefully selecting your salary to ensure you are not overpaying in payroll taxes. This is necessary as most S-Corps make the mistake of overpaying themselves and in turn overpaying in payroll taxes. Utilizing the fringe benefits discussed in this chapter and deciding which benefits will best serve you as the employee as well as your company's employees will be a great benefit in reducing the liability of the net income the S-Corp passes through to the personal tax return. If your S Corp establishes the health insurance plan for you, then the premiums can be included on your W-2 taxable wages. You'll be able to claim this deduction on your Form 1040 if you meet the following criteria. The S Corp must pay your premiums, you must correctly report the premiums on both your business and personal tax returns, and you, the S Corp owner, aren't able to receive health insurance through another employer or your spouse's employer. Additionally, you can deduct any premiums your S Corp paid for your accident insurance, dental insurance, and/or long-term care insurance. You also don't have to pay Medicare, unemployment, or Social Security taxes on the money your business pays for your health insurance. Finally, you don't have to pay taxes on any health insurance your business pays for any non-owner and non-family employees through a group health insurance policy. When your S-corporation provides your cell phone so that you can use it for business, that is a fringe benefit as well and that becomes tax-free income. If you also use that same cell phone for personal use, that's fine too. The S Corp can reimburse you for the business portion of the cost of the phone and can then deduct that amount on the corporate tax return. Providing a cell phone to employees "those children of yours that you hired" are also deductible. Another strategy that is rare but helpful is to convert your home to a rental property and save by selling it to your S Corp first. By doing this, you can avoid paying taxes on up to $250,000 of the profits from the sale (or up to $500,000 if married and filing jointly). In turn, this sale also increases your S corporation's deductions. One of my favorite strategies by far.

Regardless of the tax strategy you choose the key is making an informed decision. The saying when you know better you do better applies to your tax planning. Tax planning doesn't have to be an elaborate mathematical equation, you just need to be knowledgeable on the deductions, credits, and available expenses that are applicable to your specific tax election. The more you know the more informed decision you can make. One of the most important keys to success in your tax planning journey is to be knowledgeable and organized so that you can easily find your deductions and expenses at the time of preparation. Whether you are a do it yourselfer or your hire a professional the most important strategy is organization and recordkeeping.

Recordkeeping is key to your tax planning strategy. The law does not require any specific kind of records, but you do have to choose a recordkeeping system suited to the business that shows your income and expenses. The type of business you have affects the type of records you need to keep. You should set up a recordkeeping system using an accounting method that shows the income and expenses for the year and if there is more than one business, they should all be separated by business. The records should include a summary of all business transactions. This record is normally kept on your company's books, accounting journals and ledgers. The company's books will show the income, expenses, credits, and deductions. The business bank accounts would most likely serve as the best source of the business's books. In addition to the business bank statements, you also want to make sure you keep receipts for business purchases, payroll, and other transactions such as sales slips, paid bills, invoices, deposit slips, and cancelled checks. Examples of documents supporting the businesses' gross receipts include cash register tapes, bank deposit slips, receipt books, invoices, credit card charge slips, and Forms 1099-MISC. Documents supporting the cost of inventory may include canceled checks, cash register tape receipts, credit card sales slips, and invoices. Other expenses may be supported by canceled checks, cash register tapes, account statements, credit card sales slips, and invoices. The business needs to determine annual depreciation and the gain or loss when an asset is sold. Supporting documentation must be maintained for assets as well. That supporting documentation should show when and how the business acquired the asset, the purchase price, the cost of any improvements, the amount of any Section 179 deduction taken, deductions taken for depreciation, how the business used and disposed of the asset, the selling price, and expenses of sale. By maintaining adequate records of your books, you can avoid huge adjustments to your tax return from the IRS during examination which equates to tax savings. Business records are key to being able to verify what you put on the return vs. what is allowable and acceptable per the IRS rules.

Your business strategy for tax planning will be the standard operating procedure for your business. As the business grows, the procedure can change. You just want to make sure it is a strategy that you understand and can manage as your business continues to thrive. Depending on the tax election you choose will determine which strategy is best for the business. We've gone over a lot, I know, but I want to make sure you have all the information so that you can make an informed decision on which direction your business goes next. Based on what we've discussed you should now have a good understanding on which tax election you should be, how to properly plan for taxes throughout the year, and how to keep adequate records to substantiate all credits and deductions your business will take to lower the tax liability.

Building a Life and Business that You love

We've gone through so much during this chapter. It almost feels like we know each other. We've chosen our tax election, we've decided how we want to be taxed, we know what credits and deductions will help to reduce our tax bill, and we know how to properly plan for taxes going forward but let me ask you this. How do you build a life and business that you love, and I mean cannot do without? How do you make sure that your life is not a back seat to your business? For me it is imperative to have a work life balance. The reason I left corporate America to become an entrepreneur was to have time and freedom. Often, we devote ourselves to our business and our personal life suffers. I was so focused on being successful that I worked 7 days a week within my business and over 14 hours a day. That meant I was getting home after my children went to bed, I was missing my son's basketball games, my daughter's volleyball games, and my youngest son's soccer games. I thought this cannot be the life. This is not what I envisioned being an entrepreneur would be. Long hours, only seeing my children's faces in the mornings on the way to school, overworking myself, feeling burnt out, attitude changing because I was sleep deprived. I mean I could go on and on. Not only did I need to change my strategy for tax planning, but I also needed a new strategy to build a life and business that I loved. The first thing I did was find a support staff. I was doing everything myself, down to booking appointments, servicing the clients, marketing, networking, fixing systems as they crashed. I honestly held at least 10 positions within my own company. Once I realized I cannot do this alone, and hired a team of support staff, it was then that I could leave earlier in the day to make it home to my children. I also came to the realization that I am the owner of my life and my company therefore I choose what hours I want to work. I quickly began to live from my calendar. If my child had a game, that time was blocked off on my calendar. If I wanted to take a vacation, it was blocked off on my calendar. I made it so that I gained more control of what I do and when I do it. Since making those changes, I built a business and life that I love. I am passionate about both and had to implement changes in my day-to-day life to ensure the dream came true. I had to delegate to elevate. If I can do it, so can you!

ABOUT

Aneiia Steele is the founder of Royalty Tax Services LLC and A L S Financial Solutions. As a native of Milwaukee, WI she's seen the effects of how her community is affected by a lack of financial literacy. Aneiia's passion for educating the community on tax laws and tax strategy is what sets Aneiia apart from any other accounting agency. Her bachelor's degree which was received from Concordia University is in Criminal Justice and Accounting. Aneiia is a member and the Wisconsin Ambassador to the Association of Black Tax Professionals, a member of the National Association of Tax Professionals, a member of the IRS Annual Filing Season Program, and an

Authorized E-file provider. With 19 years of accounting experience her attention to detail and diligent research provides results to clients unlike any other agency. Aneiia partners with other tax professionals to provide an opportunity for them to start their own tax business, create passive income, and teaches her methods of success to be replicated. Aneiia believes in providing 5-star service and creating a personal experience to completely satisfy clients. Aneiia is passionate about giving back to her community; whether it is providing information, making donations, or speaking to at-risk youth she is determined to level the playing field for everyone.

Either online, or in person, we "Give Your Wallet the Royal Treatment."

Follow us on social media to stay updated: Facebook@ Royalty Tax Services LLC Instagram @ royalty_tax_services_llc

WANDA WATSON

Did you meet your goal? For most taxpayers, the annual goal is to file their tax return by the April 15th due date. Most are crossing their fingers and their toes through the process while praying there is not an excessive balance due. This is the case for the many who retain a tax preparer once a year vs retaining a tax strategist throughout the year. Retaining a tax preparer annually is likened to spending money daily with no knowledge of the end result - no idea of what it was spent on or whether there will be funds in the end to cover necessities. It's simply going through the year with little to no knowledge of the amount earned or the amount of expenses incurred to offset the actual tax liability or going through the year without determining if the correct amount of federal or state withholdings have been submitted to the revenue agencies. The realization of either is not known until the actual tax return has been filed. At that point, you're sitting with a major liability that in most cases will also accrue additional penalties and interest. Panic sets in, the fear of the unknown becomes a reality, and the end result leave many feeling baffled as to how the liability will be paid. Due to the fear of the IRS, some will begin to lose sleep at night or even incur medical conditions because of the stress the liability will create.

To some, the above scenario may seem fictitious, but I have witnessed this firsthand with clients who have come to my office seeking a resolution and/or assistance with the liability at hand. This is attributed to lack of tax planning as well as lack of budgeting but let us dig a little deeper into the differences in the processes of both and the importance of tax planning.

A typical tax preparer will receive your documents and generate your tax return. The tax preparer may or may not probe for further information to reduce your overall liability. In my experience, if you prepare your taxes with one of the well-known chains, in a number of instances, the preparer sitting across from you may have minimal experience and may be unaware of the correct questions to ask. Additionally, the focus may be to simply prepare your return with the documents provided, collect your payment, and move onto the next client. A tax preparer may or may not be accessible throughout the year if questions need to be answered pertaining to an IRS matter; however, a tax preparer is not an Enrolled Agent or CPA will not have unlimited representation rights to mediate on your behalf with the Internal Revenue Service. In summary, a tax preparer is sufficient for anyone desiring to have their tax return done swiftly and their refund received promptly.

A tax planner, often referred to as a tax strategist, is one who meets with the client at least once each quarter to review income and expenses, assists with estimated tax payments, as well as listen to the overall goals of the client. The tax strategies are structured in such a way to ensure the taxpayer's goals are achieved. Your relationship with a tax planner is generally long-term. Being accessible to clarify items in question in the event of an audit is another benefit of retaining a tax planner.

Retirement planning is a major focus and is strongly encouraged when tax planning; after all, as much as you may love what you do, making sure funds are available when you decide to take down your shingles is essential. There are a number of tax strategies available to implement while focusing on helping you attain your goals while minimizing your overall liability. While strategic tax planning enables you to avoid major tax liabilities, it does not aide in evading paying taxes. There is a difference - tax avoidance is the goal with tax planning while tax evasion is a misdemeanor and could equate to incarceration depending on the severity of the evasion. However, the only orange jumpsuit we want to see you in is that of the fashionable type.

I have a strong passion for tax planning after working with a number of business owners over the years. I've found that many business owners, especially those of color, work continually with no plan in place for retirement and nothing in place to help to leave a legacy for their children and grandchildren.

Tax planning is not a one size fits all. It is essential to consider your goals, desires, and aspirations. What are your priorities? Congratulations are definitely in order, as the best way to minimize your liability is to establish a business. The tax code is written in such a way that it favors the business owner. Therefore, you're already heading in the right direction. Are you willing to set up an office in your home used "regularly and exclusively" for business? Are you open to investing your profits? If there are opportunities for tax savings, are you willing to engage family members in your business?

Taxpayers with no business, are unable to take advantage of deductions such as business use of the home, which includes a percentage of utilities, pest control, certain repairs and maintenance, homeowners' insurance and other expenses pertaining to your home which would not otherwise be tax deductible.

With the change in the tax code in which real estate, property, state, and sales taxes paid throughout the year are now limited to a deduction of $10K, many taxpayers find they are no longer able to itemize as their itemized deductions no longer exceeds the standard deduction. Many taxpayers have left thousands of dollars on the table due to this limitation. Being able to deduct the business use of the home affords you the opportunity to itemize or take the standard deduction, in addition to using your portion of your home office expenses and is one of the many strategies to consider when tax planning.

Within the business, let us look at some of the other strategies that will help to minimize your liabilities as well as enable you take advantage of the opportunities to grow your business.

One of the first things to consider is the structure of your business. What type of entity are you? Are you a single member LLC filing a Schedule C? Are your profits generating substantial self-employment (SE) taxes in addition to your federal and state liabilities? Is it time to consider requesting to file as an S Corp? These are things to consider before making the change to an S Corp which could save you up to 50% of the Social Security and Medicare (SE) taxes you're obligated to pay as a single member LLC. Based on your revenue, can you afford to process payroll? As an S Corp, and the officer of the corporation, you would be required to run a payroll and take a "reasonable salary" each year. I strongly advise you to consult your tax planner to determine what would be deemed "reasonable" as this may be a gray area as it's a point of discussion within the IRS on a regular basis.

Health insurance is generally not deductible unless you are able to itemize, and total health expenses must exceed 7.5% of your adjusted gross income Additionally, even if you pass both of these tests it may still be excluded if you find your total itemized deductions do not exceed the standard deduction as noted above. However, if you are able to include it, the benefit in most cases is minimal. I strongly encourage all business owners to consider establishing a Health Savings Account (HSA) as well as obtaining Self Employed Health Insurance unless they or their significant other has a previously established plan in place. The number of entrepreneurs without health insurance is staggering as many have opted not to obtain health insurance because they considered it an expense they could not absorb. Seek options and take advantage of this opportunity to reduce your liability and allow your business to work for you and your family before having to calculate what's owed to the revenue agencies.

Do you have children? Are they of the age that you could reasonably document job duties and employ your child/children? I suspect you're either paying an allowance, giving money here and there for gas or for them to hang out at a movie with a friend. Why not help develop their work ethic and make payments to them that are tax deductible to you? If you can answer the previous questions in the affirmative, I encourage you to consider paying your child through your business. You will definitely be required to have a legitimate job description, one that your child can accomplish based on their age. However, the payout will be a dollar-for-dollar deduction in your business, and hence contribute to minimizing your overall liability unlike disbursing an allowance. The icing on the cake is if they can feasibly earn $13850 (up to the standard deduction) and not have a tax liability.

What about retirement? Are you where you need to be? Have you determined how much you need to have saved to live the lifestyle you desire to live when you're ready to take down your shingles from the business you've grown throughout the years? Are you contributing to a SEP, Simple, or any other investment vehicles available to you? Do you have a financial advisor that you know, like and trust? Your financial advisor and your tax strategist should know one another as they should work together and make sure their strategies are not counterproductive and you're realizing the maximum savings and profits available to you.

While it's not necessarily a tax strategy, I discuss wills with my client's as well. Is your house in order? Your will is the last love letter you can leave for your family. Help avoid the things that tear families apart upon the loss of their loved ones. At the very least, get a copy and complete "Five Wishes." Give your family the manual to inform them of your assets and your desires.

https://samaritannj.org/resources/5-wishes-living-will-documents/

These are just a few strategies to consider. However, it's essential to have your books in order throughout the year to account for all income and expenses which will enable more accurate quarterly estimated tax payments. An accurate financial statement is necessary to implement the most profitable strategies readily available.

Now, I don't want to leave you thinking there are absolutely no strategies or benefits for taxpayers without a business - the options do exist but are just not as plentiful. The beauty of it is they're also available to you in addition to the strategies implemented on the business side. Doesn't owning the business seem even more appealing at this point? Let's look at a few other deductions you and your family may be entitled to…..

The child tax credit is available to taxpayers if your main home is and the United States for more than half the year and you have a child 17 years or younger as of Dec 31 of the tax filing year. The amount of the credit is $2K but it begins to phase out at $200K if you're single and $400K if you're married.

The child and dependent care credit is another option. However, it is limited to $3K for the first child and a total of $6K for the remaining children. Note:

Dependent care includes children up to the age of 13 and individuals unable to care for themselves physically or mentally. The credit is based on a calculation and is limited to 20-35% of the amount paid. I'd strongly advise, if your employer offers pre-tax dependent care benefits, it is generally more beneficial to opt-in for the benefit than to claim it on your tax return. It would still have to be reported on the return but up to $5K can be excluded from taxable income via your employer.

The education credit is available for the student seeking higher education. The amount varies between $2K and $2500 depending on whether you're enrolled at least half time in your first four years of an undergraduate program and qualify for the American Opportunity Credit which can be as much as $2500 or if you or your dependent qualifies for the Lifetime Learning credit of $2000 which has no time limitation.

Solar panels are becoming increasingly popular. The installation of the solar panels (which can be quite costly) can net you a savings of 30% of the cost of installation via the energy credit.

Do you have your eye on a Tesla or other electric vehicle? You may qualify for a credit of up to $7500. Be mindful to talk with your tax strategist before purchasing to confirm you are below the maximum adjusted gross income if the credit is your deciding factor.

Of course, IRAs should be considered as well. Seek a financial advisor that you know, like and trust for direction on the type of IRA consider. The decision is generally based on your risk tolerance, your income, and the other vehicles in your portfolio.

As you can see, some of the credits for taxpayers with no business entity are based on formulas and there is no flexibility. The amount of credits is limited but will be considered when determining the amount of estimated tax payments due for the quarter.

In summary, a tax planner will help you make informed decisions while maximizing strategies that will benefit you and your family. Additionally, an effective tax planner will enable you to increase revenue and profits while remaining informed and implementing adjustments as needed based on any proposed changes in tax law.

ABOUT

Wanda Watson, EA, a tax strategist, is the owner and founder of Premier Business Solutions, a tax planning and accounting firm located in Chesapeake, VA, and services clients throughout the U.S. Premier Business Solution's flagship service consists of assisting elite entrepreneurs with saving thousands of dollars in taxes and increasing profits. They also provide services to include IRS negotiations, tax preparation, and out-sourced CFO services for businesses.

Wanda is licensed with the Internal Revenue Service (IRS) as an Enrolled Agent (EA). She holds an M.B.A in Accounting from Colorado Technical

University and a B.S. in Accounting from Old Dominion University.

Prior to establishing Premier Business Solutions, Wanda worked as senior staff accountant for a Virginia CPA Firm, a managing staff accountant for a Fortune 500 accounting firm as well as an Accounting Technician for the Armed Forces in Travel Disbursements, Paying and Collecting and the Air Force Commissary.

Her passion is educating six and seven figure business owners and arming taxpayers with the knowledge needed to save on taxes while remaining compliant. Premier Business Solutions also represents taxpayers who find themselves in the unfortunate situation of needing assistance mediating with the IRS - enabling them to sleep soundly at night.

As a business owner, you work tirelessly to grow your enterprise, drive profits, and navigate the complex landscape of regulations and financial responsibilities. Often overlooked in this journey, however, is a hidden treasure trove of opportunities that could significantly enhance your financial bottom line: tax credits.

Tax credits are not merely a footnote in the dense pages of tax law; they are valuable financial incentives designed to promote specific business activities, investments, and responsible practices. From fostering innovation and environmental stewardship to supporting community development and workforce growth, tax credits are vital tools that align your business goals with broader societal objectives.

This section explores different tax credits, each with unique characteristics, benefits, and requirements. These credits are scattered across various IRS forms, and most roll up to Form 3800.

General Business Credit (Form 3800)

Form 3800 is used to calculate the allowable general business credit, which is made up of several individual credits. Here's an overview of some of those credits, how they work, and general requirements or restrictions:

1. **Investment Credit (Form 3468)**
    a. What it is: Includes the Rehabilitation, Energy, and Reforestation Credits.

b. How it works: Incentive for investing in specific property, energy sources, or reforestation.

c. Documentation: Receipts, certifications, and other supporting documentation of qualifying investments.

d. Restrictions/Deadlines: Various, depending on the specific credit. May be limited based on tax liability or other factors.

2. American Samoa Economic Development Credit (Form 5735)

a. What it is: Various credits to stimulate business

investment in American Samoa.

b. How it works: Several components, including a percentage of wages paid to qualified employees.

c. Documentation: Investment records, wage records, compliance with specific requirements.

d. Restrictions/Deadlines: Must meet specific qualifications related to location, investments, and other factors.

3. Work Opportunity Credit (Form 5884)

a. What it is: Hiring individuals from certain targeted groups.

b. How it works: A percentage of the first-year wages paid to qualifying employees.

c. Documentation: Certification that the employee is a member of a targeted group, wage records.

d. Restrictions/Deadlines: Must obtain certification within 28 days of the employee's start date.

4. Research Credit (Form 6765)

a. What it is: Incentive for increasing research activities.

b. How it works: A percentage of qualifying research expenses above a base amount.

c. Documentation: Detailed records of research activities, expenses, contracts, etc.

d. Restrictions/Deadlines: Various, including limitations based on taxable income and other factors.

5. Low-Income Housing Credit (Form 8586)

a. What it is: Encouraging investment in low-income housing.

b. How it works: A percentage of the costs to build or rehabilitate low-income housing.

c. Documentation: Compliance with specific rules and regulations, including tenant income restrictions.

d. Restrictions/Deadlines: Various, including potential recapture if requirements are not met.

6. **Orphan Drug Credit (Form 8820)**

a. What it is: Incentive for clinical testing expenses for drugs for rare diseases.

b. How it works: A credit for a percentage of qualifying clinical testing expenses.

c. Documentation: Records of qualifying tests, expenditures, FDA approval, etc.

d. Restrictions/Deadlines: Various, including specific qualification requirements.

7. Disabled Access Credit (Form 8826)

a. What it is: Encouragement for making a business accessible to disabled individuals.

b. How it works: A percentage of expenditures to make a business more accessible, up to a limit.

c. Documentation: Records of qualifying expenses, including invoices and compliance with applicable laws.

d. Restrictions/Deadlines: Must comply with the Americans with Disabilities Act (ADA).

8. Qualified Plug-in Electric Vehicle Credit (Form 8834)

a. What it is: Credit for two- or three-wheeled plug-in electric vehicles.

b. How it works: A percentage of the cost of qualified vehicles, up to a limit.

c. Documentation: Purchase records, vehicle specifications.

d. Restrictions/Deadlines: Various, including specific vehicle qualifications.

9. Renewable Electricity, Refined Coal, and Indian Coal Production Credit (Form 8835)

a. What it is: Incentive for production of renewable energy and certain coal products.

b. How it works: Credit based on kilowatt-hours or tons produced and sold to an unrelated party.

c. Documentation: Detailed records of production, sales, qualifying property, etc.

d. Restrictions/Deadlines: Various, including specific qualification criteria.

10. Empowerment Zone and Renewal Community Employment Credit (Form 8844)

a. What it is: Incentive for hiring employees within empowerment zones or renewal communities.

b. How it works: A percentage of qualified wages paid to employees.

c. Documentation: Employee records, zone qualifications.

d. Restrictions/Deadlines: Specific employee and location qualifications.

11. Indian Employment Credit (Form 8845)

a. What it is: Incentive for employing members of Indian tribes.

b. How it works: A percentage of wages and healthcare costs for qualified employees.

c. Documentation: Employee qualifications, wage records.

d. Restrictions/Deadlines: Various, including tribal enrollment qualifications.

12. Credit for Employer Social Security and Medicare Taxes Paid on Certain Employee Tips (Form 8846)

a. What it is: Credit for Social Security and Medicare taxes paid on employee tips.

b. How it works: Credit for taxes paid on tips exceeding the federal minimum wage.

c. Documentation: Employee wage and tip records, tax payment records.

d. Restrictions/Deadlines: Specific industry and employee qualifications.

13. Biodiesel and Renewable Diesel Fuels Credit (Form 8864)

a. What it is: Credit for biodiesel and renewable diesel fuels production or mixing.

b. How it works: Varies based on type, production, and usage.

c. Documentation: Records of production, sales, and compliance with regulations.

d. Restrictions/Deadlines: Must meet specific criteria, including fuel type and quality standards.

14. Credit for Small Employer Pension Plan Startup Costs (Form 8881)

a. What it is: Incentive for small employers to start pension plans for employees.

b. How it works: A percentage of the costs to set up and administer the plan, up to a limit.

c. Documentation: Plan setup and administration records, compliance with regulations.

d. Restrictions/Deadlines: Must meet specific size and plan qualifications.

15. Credit for Employer-Provided Childcare Facilities and Services (Form 8882)

a. What it is: Encouragement for employer-provided childcare facilities.

b. How it works: A percentage of qualified childcare expenditures.

c. Documentation: Records of expenditures, compliance with regulations.

d. Restrictions/Deadlines: Must meet specific qualifications, including eligible childcare services.

16. Qualified Railroad Track Maintenance Credit (Form 8900)

a. What it is: Incentive for maintaining railroad tracks.

b. How it works: A percentage of qualified track maintenance expenditures.

c. Documentation: Records of maintenance work, expenditures.

d. Restrictions/Deadlines: Specific qualifications related to track ownership, type, and other factors.

17. Distilled Spirits Credit (Form 8906)

a. What it is: Credit for certain distilled spirits.

b. How it works: A specific amount per proof gallon of distilled spirits.

c. Documentation: Records of production, sales, and compliance with regulations.

d. Restrictions/Deadlines: Must meet specific criteria, including alcohol content and type.

18. Energy Efficient Home Credit (Form 8908)

a. What it is: Incentive for constructing energy-efficient homes.

b. How it works: A fixed credit for each qualified new energy-efficient home.

c. Documentation: Compliance with energy-saving criteria, certifications.

d. Restrictions/Deadlines: Various, including specific energy-efficiency requirements.

19. Alternative Motor Vehicle Credit (Form 8910)

a. What it is: Credit for purchasing alternative fuel vehicles.

b. How it works: Varies by type of vehicle and fuel efficiency.

c. Documentation: Purchase records, vehicle specifications.

d. Restrictions/Deadlines: Various, including make and model qualifications.

20. Alternative Fuel Vehicle Refueling Property Credit (Form 8911)

a. What it is: Credit for alternative fuel vehicle refueling property.

b. How it works: A percentage of the cost of qualified

alternative fuel vehicle refueling property.

c. Documentation: Records of expenditures, compliance with standards.

d. Restrictions/Deadlines: Various, including specific equipment and usage qualifications.

21. Mine Rescue Team Training Credit (Form 8923)

a. What it is: Incentive for training mine rescue team members.

b. How it works: A credit for a percentage of training program costs.

c. Documentation: Training records, compliance with standards.

d. Restrictions/Deadlines: Must meet specific qualifications, including eligible types mines.

22. Agricultural Chemicals Security Credit (Form 8931)

a. What it is: Encouragement for safeguarding agricultural chemicals.

b. How it works: A percentage of eligible costs to secure agricultural chemicals.

c. Documentation: Records of expenditures, compliance with regulations.

d. Restrictions/Deadlines: Various, including specific security measures.

23. Credit for Employer Differential Wage Payments (Form 8932)

a. What it is: Credit for employers who pay differential wages to employees serving in the military.

b. How it works: A percentage of the differential wage payments.

c. Documentation: Wage records, military orders.

d. Restrictions/Deadlines: Specific employee qualifications, including length and type of service.

24. Carbon Dioxide Sequestration Credit (Form 8933)

a. What it is: Incentive for carbon capture and sequestration.

b. How it works: A credit per metric ton of qualified carbon dioxide sequestered.

c. Documentation: Records of capture, sequestration, compliance with regulations.

d. Restrictions/Deadlines: Various, including specific qualifications and methods.

25. Biodiesel and Renewable Diesel Fuels Credit (Form 8864)

a. What it is: Credit for biodiesel and renewable diesel fuels production or mixing.

b. How it works: Varies based on type, production, and usage.

c. Documentation: Records of production, sales, and compliance with regulations.

d. Restrictions/Deadlines: Must meet specific criteria, including fuel type and quality standards.

26. Credit for Small Employer Pension Plan Startup Costs (Form 8881)

a. What it is: Incentive for small employers to start pension plans for employees.

b. How it works: A percentage of the costs to set up and administer the plan, up to a limit.

c. Documentation: Plan setup and administration records, compliance with regulations.

d. Restrictions/Deadlines: Must meet specific size and plan qualifications.

27. Low Sulfur Diesel Fuel Production Credit (Form 8896)

a. What it is: Incentive for producing low sulfur diesel fuel.

b. How it works: A specific amount per gallon of qualified fuel.

c. Documentation: Production records, compliance with standards.

d. Restrictions/Deadlines: Various, including specific sulfur content qualifications.

28. Credit for Employer Differential Wage Payments (Form 8932)

a. What it is: Credit for employers who pay differential wages to employees serving in the military.

b. How it works: A percentage of the differential wage payments.

c. Documentation: Wage records, military orders.

d. Restrictions/Deadlines: Specific employee qualifications, including length and type of service.

29. Qualified Plug-in Electric Drive Motor Vehicle Credit (Form 8936)

a. What it is: Credit for purchasing qualified plug-in electric drive motor vehicles.

b. How it works: Varies by type, battery capacity, and other factors.

c. Documentation: Purchase records, vehicle specifications.

d. Restrictions/Deadlines: Various, including make and model qualifications.

30. Credit for Small Employer Health Insurance Premiums (Form 8941)

a. What it is: Encouragement for small employers to provide health insurance to employees.

b. How it works: A percentage of premiums paid for employee health insurance.

c. Documentation: Premium payment records, employee coverage details.

d. Restrictions/Deadlines: Specific size, coverage, and employee qualifications.

Here are a few more general categories and special situations you might encounter:

31. Distilled Spirits Credit

a. What it is: Credit related to the production and distribution of distilled spirits.

b. How it works: Specific qualifications and amounts tied to production quantities.

c. Documentation: Production records, compliance with relevant regulations.

d. Restrictions/Deadlines: Various, including specific qualifications regarding production type and scale.

32. Nonconventional Source Fuel Credit

a. What it is: Incentive for producing fuel from nonconventional sources.

b. How it works: Specific amount per barrel (or equivalent) of qualified fuel.

c. Documentation: Production records, compliance with energy standards.

d. Restrictions/Deadlines: Specific qualifications related to fuel type and production methods.

33. Energy Efficient Appliance Credit

a. What it is: Credit for the production of energy-efficient appliances.

b. How it works: Amounts vary based on the type and efficiency of the appliance.

c. Documentation: Compliance with energy-saving criteria, certifications.

d. Restrictions/Deadlines: Specific energy efficiency requirements.

34. Alternative Motor Vehicle Credit

a. What it is: Incentive for purchasing alternative fuel vehicles.

b. How it works: Varies by type and fuel efficiency.

c. Documentation: Purchase records, vehicle specifications.

d. Restrictions/Deadlines: Various, including make and model qualifications.

35. Carbon Dioxide Sequestration Credit

a. What it is: Credit for carbon capture, utilization, and sequestration.

b. How it works: Amount based on metric tons of qualified carbon dioxide.

c. Documentation: Sequestration records, compliance with environmental regulations.

d. Restrictions/Deadlines: Specific qualifications related to sequestration methods and amounts.

36. Qualified Film or Television Production Credit

a. What it is: Incentive for qualified film or television productions.

b. How it works: Specific qualifications and amounts tied to production costs and locations.

c. Documentation: Production records, expenditures, location compliance.

d. Restrictions/Deadlines: Specific qualifications regarding production type, costs, and other factors.

ABOUT THE COMPILER

Dr. Cozette M. White is an acclaimed 6x bestselling authors, nationally recognized tax & accounting strategist, international speaker, real estate investor and philanthropist.

Serving clients for 25 years, Dr. White has been coined "Your Financial Physician" as a result of her unparalleled ability to empower her clients to ditch debt and develop a plan to create the kind of wealth that leaves a secure financial legacy.

Dr. White is the award-winning CEO of My Financial Home Enterprises®, a certified woman-owned firm providing tax, accounting and business management services. In 2019, Dr. White founded The Tax Curative Institute® to empower and support tax professionals. The institution is an IRS approved continuing education (CE) provider for Enrolled Agents, Credentialed Tax Preparers, and Non-Credentialed Tax Preparers delivering high quality educational courses coupled with a powerful easy to use learning platform.

Dr. White is the resident Money Matter's Tax Expert for FOX40. Her excellent media credentials, professionalism, and outgoing personality has allowed her to provide expert advice on tax issues for CBS This Morning, NBC, ABC and FOX television stations. She has been featured on the numerous radio shows including Radio One and iHeart radio, she's a recurring voice to millions making regular appearances in various national media outlets, including Black Enterprise, Forbes, Women of Wealth, Upscale, The Huffington Post, and countless newspapers across the country. In 2017, Dr. White was awarded the Lifetime Achievement Award by President Barack Obama.

Dr. Cozette M. White has been awarded a Doctorate Degree of Philosophy Letters, a Masters of Business

Administration and a Bachelor of Science degree in Accounting.

Dr. Cozette has been an IRS Tax Practitioner since 1991 and an Electronic Return Originator (ERO) since 2001 and she's a CTEC Registered Tax Preparer (CRTP).

She is involved in her community and is a member of Alpha Kappa Alpha Sorority, Inc; she is a member of the National Association of Black Accountants, National Black MBA Association and Association of Black Tax Professionals and she is also the California Ambassador for the Association of Black Tax Professionals, where she provides mentorship and assistance to other black tax professionals alongside other state Ambassadors.

Dr. Cozette's personal and professional achievements have not gone unnoticed, and through the years she has been awarded:

- 2020 Top 31 Women of Dignity – History Makers by K.I.S.H. Magazine
- 2019 Productive Business Community Game Changer Award
- 2019 Women Add Value Leadership Recognition Award
- 2019 Top 28 Influential Business Pioneer by K.I.S.H. Magazine
- 2019 Dynasty of Dreamers by K.I.S.H. Magazine

- 2018 Top Business Award by The Boss Network
- 2018 Top Female Expert by Huff Post
- 2017 Top Business Award by The Boss Network
- 2017 Lifetime Achievement Award by President Barack Obama
- 2017 10 Women Speakers To Know - Jazzy Creative Magazine
- 2017 Top 6 Leaders of The Month - WomELLE Magazine
- 2016 Wealth Builder Extraordinaire by Women of Wealth Magazine

AUTHOR DIRECTORY

Aneiia "Your Trailblazing Tax Unicorn" Steele
Royalty Tax Services LLC, CEO and Founder
www.royaltytaxservicesllc.com
info@royaltytaxservicesllc.com
(414) 885-4150

Patrice Jones
Email
patricejones@patricejonesassociates.com
Website
www.patricejonesandassociates.com

Shakeemah Murray
Assured Accounting & Associates
www.AAandAssoc.com
Shakeemah@AssuredAccountingandAsso.com

Wanda Watson
Premier Business Solutions
Enrolled Agent

www.premierbusinessstrategist.com
wanda@premierbusinessstrategist.com

(757) 410-8030

Contact:

Dr. Cozette M White

(805) 983-1151

www.myfinancialhome.com

info@myfinancialhome.com

www.ingramcontent.com/pod-product-compliance
Lightning Source LLC
Chambersburg PA
CBHW072303210326
41519CB00057B/2601

* 9 7 9 8 9 8 8 5 1 8 2 2 8 *